DISPUTES REVIEWED

DISPUTES REVIEWED

In a sermon, preached at the Evening
Lecture, at Salters Hall, on Lord's Day,
July 23RD, 1710

❧

REV. MATTHEW HENRY
MINISTER OF THE GOSPEL IN CHESTER

CURIOSMITH
MINNEAPOLIS

Published by Curiosmith.
Minneapolis, Minnesota.
Internet: curiosmith.com.

The text of this edition is from *The Miscellaneous Works of the Rev. Matthew Henry*, published by ROBERT CARTER & BROTHERS, 1855.

The "Guide to the Contents" was added to this edition by the publisher.

ISBN 9781946145185

GUIDE TO THE CONTENTS

DISPUTES REVIEWED

What was it that ye disputed among yourselves by the way?—MARK 9:33.

Our Lord Jesus is here calling his disciples to an account about a warm debate they happened to have among themselves, as they travelled along, upon a question often started, but not yet determined, *Which of them should be the greatest?* They thought no other but that their Master should shortly enter upon the possession of a temporal kingdom, and all the pomp and grandeur of it, and they should be preferred with him; but they could not agree who should be prime-minister of state, and have the first post of honor. It is a sad instance of the remainders of corruption in the hearts even of good people; and shows that pride, ambition, and affectation of worldly honor, are sins that do most easily beset even Christ's own disciples; which, therefore, we should all carefully watch and strive against.

Probably our Lord Jesus overheard some words that passed in this dispute; for those who are hot upon an argument are apt to speak louder than becomes them; and when the temper is not kept within due bounds, commonly the voice is not. But whether he overheard them or no, he knew very well what they had been talking of, and every word that had been said, and, which was more than any *man* could know, from what principle it was said, and what more they would have said; for as there is not a word in our tongue, so there is not a thought in our heart, though newly risen and started there, though industriously suppressed and stifled there, but he knows it altogether.[1] He is that essential, eternal Word of God, who is a discerner of the thoughts and intents of the heart, and before whom all things are naked and open.[2] Let all the churches take notice of this, That our Lord Jesus not only knows our work, but is he who searches the reins and hearts.[3]

And yet though Christ knew what his disciples had been talking of, he asked them what it was, because he would know it from *them*, and would have them to confess their fault and folly in it; that from thence he might take occasion to rectify their mistakes, and to instruct and reason them into a better temper.

1　Psalm 139:4.
2　Hebrews 4:12, 13.
3　Revelation 2:19, 23.

Think not that my design from this text is to arraign, examine, or inquire into any disputes or contests that may be among you, of any kind; for as (blessed be God) I know of no *particular* occasion for it, nor have any thing else in my eye, in the choice of this subject, but what is *common to all;* so if there were, I should think myself the unfittest man in the world to be a judge or a divider. And besides, if I should thus go about to take my Master's work out of his hands, I should contradict that which is my design—in putting this question to you, *What was it that you disputed among yourselves by the way?*—and that is, to show you that our blessed Lord Jesus does and will inquire into these matters, and bind you over to his judgment.

Four things this text teaches us, who are all in profession *disciples* of Christ, as we are baptized Christians.

I. That we must all expect to be called to an account by our Lord Jesus.

II. That we must, in a particular manner, be called to an account about our discourses among ourselves.

III. That, among our discourses, we shall especially be called to an account about our disputes.

IV. That, of all our disputes, we shall be most strictly reckoned with for our disputes about precedency and superiority.

I. We must all expect to be called to an account

shortly, by our Lord Jesus, concerning the temper of our minds, and the course and tenor of our lives, now we are *in the way*.

1. We are all now *in the way*, following Christ, as his disciples here, in *consort*. We are *viatores—travellers*, under the conduct of our great Master, towards the better country. And here we are upon trial; it is the state of our probation; and according as our steps are, while we are in the way, our rest will be when we are at our journey's end. It concerns us therefore, what we have to do, to do it while we are yet in the way;[1] and whatever we do while we are in the way, to do it with an eye to our end.

2. There will be a review of what passes *in the way;*[2] it will all be called over again; every work and every word will be brought into judgment, will be weighed in a just and unerring balance, will be produced in evidence for us or against us. There will not need any repetition, every thing is now recorded in the book of God's omniscience; and it is enough that, in that day, the *books will be opened*, and all will be *judged out of those things which were* found *written in the books, according to their works*.[3] It concerns us therefore, whatever we do *in the way*, to do it as those who must give account, and to consider how it will pass in the account; how it will

---

1 Matthew 5:25.
2 Ecclesiastes 12:14.
3 Revelation 20:12.

look in the review; that we may dread doing that which will make against us then, and may abound in that which will be *fruit abounding to our account*,[1] and which we shall meet again with comfort, on the other side death and the grave.

3. The account in the great day must be given up to our Lord Jesus, for we call him *Master and Lord*, as these disciples did; and to him therefore we are accountable, as *scholars* and *servants*, how we spend our time. He is our Judge, for he is our Law-giver;[2] and to him the Father has committed all judgment,[3] particularly that in which he will judge the world in righteousness by that man whom he has ordained.[4] Christ shall have the honor of it, and let all good Christians take the comfort of it, that he who is an advocate for all believers will be their judge: but withal, let it oblige us to the utmost care and circumspection in our walking: we must therefore labor to be accepted of the Lord, and approve ourselves to him in our integrity, because we shall all appear before the judgment-seat of Christ,[5] to give account of every thing done in the body. God made the world, by his Son; and by him, as the fittest person, he will judge the world.

---

1 Philippians 4:17.
2 Isaiah 33:22.
3 John 5:22.
4 Acts 17:31.
5 2 Corinthians 5:9, 10.

Now this is a good reason,

(1.) Why we should judge ourselves, and prove our own work, and see that our matters be right and good against that day. Let us examine ourselves concerning our spiritual state, that we may make sure work for our own souls; and often call ourselves to an account concerning the way we are in, and the steps we take in that way, that we may renew our repentance for whatever we find to have been amiss, and make our peace with God in Christ. And *if we would* thus *judge ourselves, we should not be judged*[1] of the Lord. When we come to our journey's end, it will be asked, how we carried ourselves *in the way*. Let us therefore carry ourselves accordingly, and *ponder the path of our feet*.

(2.) It is a good reason why we should not judge one another, or be severe in our censures one of another: we thereby invade Christ's throne, for it is his prerogative to call his disciples to an account; and though he designed them to be one another's helpers, he never intended they should be one another's judges. *We must all stand before the judgment-seat of Christ*, and therefore must not judge one another. We must be judged ourselves; and may expect to be judged with severity, if we be severe in judging our brethren, for the measure we mete will be measured to us.[2] Our brethren likewise must be judged

1 1 Corinthians 11:31.
2 Matthew 7:1, 2.

by the Lord Jesus, and, therefore, if we pretend to judge them, they are *coram non judice—before a judge without authority*. Who are we that we should judge another man's servant? *to his own master he stands or falls*,[1] and to his judgment it is fit we should leave him.

II. Among other things that pass *in the way*, we must expect to be called to account for what we have talked *among ourselves*. We are apt to make a light matter of this; and when we have talked at random, what comes uppermost, without regard to God or man, we think to turn it off with an excuse that it was but talk, and *words are but wind:* but we wretchedly mistake, and put a cheat upon ourselves, if that be true which our Saviour has told us, and undoubtedly true it is, that not only for every profane and wicked word, for every false and spiteful word, but *for every idle word that men speak*, they must *give account in the day of judgment;* nay, and so shall their doom be, for by thy words thou shalt be justified, and by thy words thou shalt be condemned.[2] Christ takes notice of what we say, now; and we should think we hear him say to us when we are in conversation, as he did to the two disciples going to Emmaus, *What manner of communications are these that ye have one to another, as ye walk and are sad*,[3] or, as ye sit and are merry? Are they such as

1 Romans 14:4.
2 Matthew 12:36, 37.
3 Luke 24:17.

become Christians? Are you not saying that which must be unsaid again by repentance, or you will be undone? And as Christ takes notice of it now, so he will call it over again in the day of account.

What we talk *among ourselves* with the usual freedom of conversation we do not expect to hear of again; it is *inter nos—between ourselves,* and therefore we think we may allow ourselves a liberty. What is said under the seal of conversation, we think almost as safe in point of honor, as what is said under the seal of confession; none but a talebearer, that great mischief-maker, will reveal such secrets;[1] but though it be talked *among ourselves,* it cannot escape either the cognizance or the judgment of our Lord Jesus.

1. If we talk any thing which is good among ourselves, and which is to the use of edifying;[2] which manifests grace in the speaker, and ministers grace to the hearers; Christ takes notice of that, and we shall hear of it again to our comfort, in that day when those who thus confess Christ before men[3] shall be owned by him before his Father, and the holy angels. When they who *feared the Lord spake often one to another,* for their mutual encouragement to hold fast their integrity in a time of general apostasy, *The Lord hearkened and heard it,* as one

---

1 Proverbs 11:13.

2 Ephesians 4:29.

3 Matthew 10:32.

greatly well pleased with it, and *a book of remembrance was written before him*, in which were entered all those pious conferences *of them that feared the Lord, and thought upon his name;*[1] and the day will come when this book, among the rest, shall be opened.

There is not a good word coming from a good heart, and directed to a good end, but it is heard in secret, and shall be rewarded openly, though, perhaps, there are those now who ridicule and banter such language. What is spoken for the edification of others, will turn to a good account to ourselves: and it will add to our joy in heaven, to have been any way instrumental to help others thither. Nay, if it should not reach their hearts for whom it is designed, yet the comfort of it will return into our own bosoms; and what was well intended for the honor of Christ, shall not be overlooked in the day of account.

This should engage and encourage us to keep up religious discourse, that it will be remembered to our advantage in the accounts shortly, though we may forget it; as the righteous could not say that ever they saw Christ hungry, and fed him, or thirsty, and gave him drink;[2] yet Christ will not forget it, but will place it to account, as an acceptable service done to him.

---

1 Malachi 3:16.
2 Matthew 25:37.

2. If we talk any thing that is ill among ourselves; if any corrupt communication proceeds out of our mouths, dictated by the corruption of our minds, and which has a tendency to corrupt the minds and manners of others; Christ observes that too, is displeased with it—and we shall hear of it again, either by the checks of our own consciences, in order to our repentance, or in the day of the revelation of the righteous judgment of God, when, according to Enoch's prophecy, the Lord shall come[1] to reckon with sinners, not only for all their ungodly deeds, but for all their hard speeches, spoken against him. It will be asked sooner or later, What was it that you said such a time, proudly, vainly, filthily, that foolish talking and jesting which is not becoming? What was it that you said in such and such company by way of reproach to your neighbor, when you sat deliberately, sat magisterially, and spoke against your brother, and slandered those,[2] whose good names you ought to have protected? or, which aggravates it, by way of reflection on your superiors; reviling the gods, and speaking evil of the rulers of your people,[3] little thinking that a bird of the air may carry the voice?[4] Let this consideration oblige us all to take heed to our ways, that we offend not

---

1 Jude 15.
2 Psalm 50:20.
3 Exodus 22:28.
4 Ecclesiastes 10:20.

with our tongue, and to keep our mouth as it were with a bridle,[1] that we may say nothing but what we can bear to be told of again. And we have need to beg of God, that by his grace he would *set a watch before the door of our lips*,[2] a double watch upon the door of our hearts, *out of the abundance of which the mouth speaks*, that nothing may proceed from them to his dishonor.

III. As our other discourses *among ourselves by the way*, so especially our disputes, will all be called over again, and we shall be called to an account about them. *What was it that ye disputed among yourselves?* What was the subject of the dispute? and how was it managed? Disputing supposes some variance and strife, and a mutual contradiction and opposition arising from it. Disputing by the way is falling out by the way, a thing directly contrary to the charge which Joseph, as a type of Christ, gave to his brethren, *See that ye fall not out by the way;*[3] and therefore we may expect to be reproved for it.

There are disputes that are of use among the disciples of Christ, and which in the review we may reflect upon with comfort. Did we dispute—For the conviction of atheists and deists, and other the enemies of our holy religion; or for the confirmation of those who were in danger of being drawn

1 Psalm 39:1.
2 Psalm 141:3.
3 Genesis 45:24.

away by their delusions? Did we contend earnestly
for the faith once delivered to the saints,[1] and with
meekness and fear both instruct others that oppose
themselves,[2] and give a reason of our own hope that
is in us?[3] Did we, fairly and calmly, discuss lesser
matters in difference between us and our brethren,
that we might find out the truth, and have our mistakes rectified; or, if we cannot, hereby, come to be
of the same mind, yet we may see that even those
we differ from have so much color of reason on
their side, as that they may still differ from us, and
yet not forfeit their reputation either for wisdom
or honesty? Did we, with prudence and mildness,
debate our cause with our neighbor himself, and
not go forth hastily to strive;[4] did we tell him his
fault between us and him alone,[5] before we told it
to the world or the church, in order to a friendly
accommodation? These are disputes which will pass
well in the account, when they come to be called
over again.

But our disputes are too often such, that when
we come to be asked about them, as the disciples
were here, we shall, like them, hold our peace, as
being ashamed to have them spoken of again, and

1 Jude 3.
2 2 Timothy 2:25.
3 1 Peter 3:15.
4 Proverbs 25:8, 9.
5 Matthew 18:15.

having nothing to say in our own vindication: and (as the town-clerk of Ephesus apprehended) when we are called in question for the uproar, can show no justifiable cause, whereby we may give an account of it.[1]

Three things may occasion disputes among Christians, among ministers, neighbors, friends, relations, which, perhaps, when they come to be reflected upon, as here, will be found to have a great deal in them that was culpable: different opinions, separate interests, and clashing humors.

1. Disputes commonly arise from *difference of opinion*, either in religion and divine things; (about which oftentimes the disputes and contests are most violent) or in philosophy, politics, or other parts of learning; or in the conduct of human life. While men differ so much in capacity, temper, genius, and education, and different sentiments are received by tradition from our fathers, it cannot be expected that men should all agree in the same notions. The same thing seen with different eyes, and by different lights, may appear to one true and very good, and to another false and very bad, though both employ their faculties about it with equal diligence and sincerity. This cannot but give rise to disputes, for we are naturally forward (and sometimes over-forward) to clear ourselves, and convince others; and have such a conceit of our own judgment, as to think

1 Acts 19:40.

that every body ought to be of one mind, and that if they will be ruled by reason, they will be so: for vain man would be wise, would be thought to be so, though he be born as the wild ass's colt.[1]

But these disputes are often such as we may justly be ashamed of, when we come to look back upon them.

(1.) Upon account of the matter of them. What was it that we disputed among ourselves? What was it we were so hot and eager about?

Perhaps it was something *above us*, about the nature and attributes, the counsels and decrees, of God; and the operations of his providence and grace; and the person of the Mediator: those *secret* things which belong not to us:[2] things which we did not understand, nor could: things which it was presumption for us to dispute about; for the angels with an awful reverence humbly desire to look into them,[3] as not pretending to be masters of them. And the great apostle, who had been in the third heavens, not only owned that the words he heard there were unspeakable,[4] but was so much at a loss to express himself concerning the work of redemption, though it is in some measure revealed, that despairing to find the bottom, he sits down at the

---

1 Job 11:12.
2 Deuteronomy 29:29.
3 1 Peter 1:12.
4 2 Corinthians 12:4.

brink, and adores the depth of that mystery: *O the depth of the wisdom and knowledge of God!*[1] O what reason have we with Job to abhor ourselves, and to repent in dust and ashes, because, like him, in our disputes with our friends,[2] concerning the reasons and methods of God's proceedings, we have darkened counsel by words without knowledge; and have uttered that which we understood not, things too wonderful for us.

Perhaps it was something *below us*, not worth disputing about, especially, with so much warmth and violence: it was a trifle, a mere strife of words,[3] a dispute *de lana caprina—about a thing of no value;* as if the matter were started only for want of something to wrangle about; so inconsiderable a thing, that which way soever it goes, the costs are much more than the damage. In the reflection, we may justly blush to think that we should make so much ado, so great a noise, about nothing.

Perhaps it was something *foreign to us*, that we were no way concerned in; some matter of politics it may be, which belongs not to those of our rank and station, but must be left to wiser heads, whose business it is to deal in things of that nature. Our Lord Jesus after his resurrection twice checked his disciples for a vain curiosity—once in inquiring

---

1 Romans 11:33.
2 Job 42:3, 6.
3 1 Timothy 6:4.

concerning one another's affairs; when Peter asked concerning John, *What shall this man do?* Christ answered him, *What is that to thee? Follow thou me?*[1]—and another time in inquiring concerning God's counsels, *It is not for you to know the times or the seasons.*[2]

Perhaps it was something *indifferent;* like the controversy among the primitive Christians concerning the observing of days, and making a distinction of meats,[3] which the apostle himself does not think fit to determine, but leaves each side to practice according as their judgment was, without imposing upon either, since they might be of either mind, and yet be accepted of God; only he forbids them to fall out about it, or to despise or Judge one another.

(2.) Upon account of our management of them. When our disputes among ourselves by the way come to be reviewed, it will be found that the mischief was done not by the things themselves, concerning which we differed, but by our mismanagement of the controversy.

Our Master will be displeased with us if it be found that we have been hot and fierce in our disputes, and have mingled our passions and peevish resentments with them; if a point of honor has

---

1 John 21:22.
2 Acts 1:7.
3 Romans 14:2 etc.

governed us more than a point of conscience, and we have contended more for victory and reputation; than for truth and duty; if we have contended about things of small moment for, or against, them, and have neglected the weightier matters of the law and gospel; if we have spent more of our zeal on matters in difference than they deserve; and have lost the vitals of religion, in our heat about circumstantials, and have disputed away our seriousness and devotion, *What then shall we do when God riseth up? and when he visiteth, what shall we answer him?*[1]

If in our disputes for the truth, we lie against the truth, and *speak deceitfully for God*, the good intention will be so far from justifying the lie, that the lie will condemn the good intention, and convict it of hypocrisy; for if the intention were really good, such a practice would be abhorred. If we have the itch of disputing, and a spirit of contradiction, that is certainly one of those foolish hurtful lusts, from whence come wars and fightings. If we receive our brethren who are weak *to doubtful disputations;*[2] and love to perplex and puzzle them, and run them aground with objections against what they and we believe; it shows a great contempt both of the truth and of their souls, and is a jesting with both. If we judge, and censure, and condemn our brethren who are not in every thing of our mind, and though

1 Job 31:14.
2 Romans 14:1.

we call ourselves disciples, set up for masters, many masters;[1] if we give reproachful language, and call foul names, which commonly betrays the weakness of the cause, and is ingloriously pressed into the service to make up the deficiency of argument; we shall have a great deal to answer for, when all our disputes shall be called over again by our Master.

2. Many disputes arise from *separate and interfering interests in this world.* Neighbors and relations quarrel about their rights and properties, their estates and trades, their honors and powers and pleasures; *Meum* and *Tuum—My rent* and *Thy bond,* are the great subjects of dispute, and engage people in endless strifes. The first dispute we read of in the primitive church was about a money matter; the Grecians quarrelled with the Hebrews *because* they thought their *widows were neglected in the daily ministration.*[2] Many disputes of this kind happen, which will be inquired into as well as those about differences in opinion; and therefore it concerns us to reflect upon them, that whatever we find to have been amiss in them may be repented of.

We may, in godly sorrow, quarrel with *ourselves,* and justly, for our unjust, unbecoming quarrels with *our brethren:*

Ask then—What was it that you disputed about with such a neighbor, or such a friend, at such a time?

---

1 James 3:1.
2 Acts 6:1.

Perhaps you disputed that which you ought to have yielded without dispute, a just debt or a rightful possession, which you thought to have carried, by dint of opposition, against equity. Perhaps you disputed about something very trivial, and of small value, which was not worth controverting, but which if the right were indeed of your side, you might have receded from it for peace' sake, without any detriment to yourselves or families. Perhaps the dispute might have been prevented, or when it was began, might quickly and easily have been accommodated, with a little wisdom and love; as the strife between Abraham and Lot was soon ended, and the matter compromised by Abraham's prudent condescension.[1] A little yielding would pacify great offenses, and put an effectual stop to that threatening mischief which sometimes a little fire kindles.

Review your lawsuits. And it may be you will find, that how stiff soever you were in the heat of the prosecution of them, your cooler thoughts tell you they were not managed as become Christians; you did not try to end things, as you ought to have done, in an amicable way. Perhaps they were begun rashly, and in passion; and then no wonder if they be carried on unfairly, and that which was a hasty, sudden passion in the beginning of the quarrel, is in danger of ripening into a rooted malice before the end of it, and they who at first pretended that

1 Genesis 13:8, 9.

they designed only to *right themselves*, at length, as their resentments have grown more and more keen, are not ashamed to own that they are resolved to *avenge themselves.*

These disputes, as they are most common, so they are most scandalous, among relations, and those who are under particular obligations to love one another. And whatever keeps brethren from dwelling together in unity, is very provoking to Christ, who has made brotherly love the livery of his family: and it is very hardly removed: for a *brother offended is harder to be won than a strong city, and their contentions are as the door of a castle;*[1] witness Jacob and Esau.

3. Some disputes, and hot ones too, arise merely from *passion and clashing humors*, where really there is nothing of judgment or interest in the case. Some indulge themselves in a crossness of temper, that makes them continually uneasy to their relations, the nearest, the dearest, and to all about them. They love to thwart and disagree, and to dispute every thing, though ever so plain, or ever so trifling. Many make their lives, and the relations wherein they stand, uncomfortable by this; especially when both sides are of such a spirit: one will have their humor, their saying, and the other will have theirs, and so they are ever and anon disputing which shall be greatest, and instead of aiming to please, are

1 Proverbs 18:19.

contriving to displease and contradict one another.

But do such consider, that they must give an account to Christ for all these *disputes among themselves by the way;* that they will all be called over again? How ill does it become the disciples and followers of the humble Jesus to carry things with a high hand, imperiously and with rigor, toward their inferior relations; not suffering them to speak for themselves, nor willing to hear reason from them. How ill does it become the worshippers of the God of love to be envious, and spiteful, and ill-natured, and quarrelsome with all they have any dealings with! The father of the prodigal, when his elder son was out of humor, angry, and would not come in, did not dispute with him, chide him, and threaten him, though he very well deserved it; but he went out and entreated him,[1] spoke to him smoothly, and so brought him into good temper again; which is written for our *learning*, that we may go and do likewise, but withal for our *shame* that we have not done so. By the account which the Scripture gives of some peevish passionate disputes, it appears that notice is taken of the height to which the ferment of the spirit rises at such a time. When the men of Ephraim quarrelled with Gideon upon a point of honor, it is left upon record, that they did *chide with him sharply*,[2] though by his exemplary mildness, as

1 Luke 15:28.
2 Judges 8:9.

well as by his eminent services, he deserved better at
their hands. When, in a like case, Judah and Israel
fell out, it is observed, that *the words of the men
of Judah were fiercer than the words of the men of
Israel.*[1] And if it be so indeed, that an account is
kept of the sharpness of our chiding, and the fierce-
ness of our words, we are concerned by true repentance to judge ourselves for it, that we may not be
judged of the Lord.

And whatever we find has been amiss in our disputes of any kind, let it be amended for the future.

(1.) As far as we are able to make a judgment, let
us see to it that we have truth and right on our side,
in all our disputes, and not be confident any farther
than we see just cause to be so. We must not only
never contend for that which we know to be false
and wrong, but also never for that which is doubtful, or which we do not know to be true and right.
Let us not wrong our consciences in any of our contests; nor say we believe that to be true, and therefore dispute for it, which really we do not believe
to be so; nor demand that *as* our own, which we
know or have reason to suspect we have no good
title to; nor deny that to another which we cannot
but think is justly his.

And if, in the progress of any dispute or controversy, it be made to appear to us, at length, that we
were mistaken, and in the wrong, we must be ready

1 2 Samuel 19:43.

to acknowledge it, thankful to those who have discovered it to us, and not ashamed to let fall the controversy. And we have a false notion of honor, if we think this will be any real disparagement to us; for certainly St. Paul showed more true courage; and merited more true praise, when he said, *I can do nothing against the truth,*[1] than Goliath did, when he defied all the armies of Israel.

(2.) In matters of doubtful disputation: while we are contending for that which we take to be right, let us at the same time think it possible that we may be in the wrong. When we contend for the great principles of religion, in which all good Christians are agreed, we need not fear our being in a mistake; they are of undoubted certainty, *We know and are sure that Jesus is the Christ.* But there are many things that are not so clearly revealed, because not of so much moment, in which the truth indeed lies but on one side, and yet wise and good men are not agreed on which side it lies. Here, though we both argue and act according to the light that God has given us, yet we must not be over-confident of our own judgment, as if wisdom must die with us. Others have understanding as well as we, and are not inferior to us;[2] nay, perhaps, they every way excel us, and, therefore, who can tell but they may be in the right? However, they argue and act according to

1 2 Corinthians 13:8.
2 Job 12:2.

the light they have, which we ought to pay a defer-
ence to, so as not to condemn all those for weak
men, or bad men, who are not in every thing of our
mind, and will not say as we say. Job in dispute is not
unwilling to put the case, *Be it that I have erred.*[1]

In matters of fact on which right depends, it is
possible we may be mistaken; *Humanum est errare—
to err is human.* Words may be misunderstood and
misapprehended; and the wisest, and most cautious
and observing, may be guilty of an oversight, and
may forget something that would very much alter the
case; and, therefore, it will be no credit to our wisdom
and goodness to be too positive, too peremptory, as
long as there is a possibility of our being deceived.
Never let our assertions go beyond our assurances,
nor let us give that as certain and great, which was
given us doubtful and little; but be very wary in what
we maintain, not only for our reputation's sake, lest
our neighbor search us and put us to shame, but for
conscience' sake, toward God, who hates a proud
look, and a lying tongue;[2] two very bad things, that
commonly go together, to support one another.

(3.) Let us keep the full possession and govern-
ment of our own spirits, in all our disputes. Let us
carefully suppress all inward tumults, whatever prov-
ocation may be given us; and let our minds be calm
and sedate, whatever argument we are engaged in.

1 Job 19:4.
2 Proverbs 6:17.

Let no contradiction put us into a heat or disorder; for when passion is up, we are not so capable as we ought to be, either to hear reason or to speak it, nor is it likely we should either convince or be convinced of truth and right. Meekness and mildness of spirit do as much befriend a cause, as they are the beauty and ornament of its advocates.

If we contend for that which is wrong, the more passionate we are, the greater is the sin of the contention, and the more there is of the image of the devil upon it, who is not only the *father of lies* and falsehoods, but a *red dragon*, and a *roaring lion*. But if we have truth and right on our side, that needs no intemperate heats and passions for the support of it, nor can have any real service done it by them. The cause of heaven can never be pleaded with any credit or success by a tongue set on fire of hell. *The wrath of man works not the righteousness of God.*[1] Parties may be served by fury and violence, but the common interests of pure Christianity will certainly be prejudiced by it. Christ was therefore fit to teach us, and we are invited to come and learn of him, it is not said, because *in him were hid all the treasures of wisdom and knowledge,*[2] though that is certainly true, but *because he is meek and lowly in heart,*[3] *and can have compassion on the ignorant;*

---

1 James 1:20.
2 Colossians 2:3.
3 Matthew 11:29.

and herein all who undertake to instruct others must study to imitate him. And this is the likeliest way to gain our point, if indeed we be in the right; for *the words of the wise are heard in quiet, more than the cry of him that rules among fools!*[1]

(4.) Let us never lose the charity we ought to have for our brethren in our disputes of any kind, nor violate the sacred laws of it. Our Lord Jesus foresaw, and foretold, that the preaching of his gospel would occasion much division, that it would set men at variance,[2] and be the subject of much dispute; and therefore he thought it very requisite to bind the command of mutual love so much the more strongly upon his followers, because there was danger lest it should be lost in these disputes: he makes it one of the fundamental laws of his kingdom, the *new commandment, That we love one another;* and the livery of his family, by which all men might know who are his disciples. *See how these Christians love one another.*

Let us, therefore, in all our disputes keep ourselves under the commanding power and influence of holy love; for that victory is dearly purchased, that is obtained at the expense of Christian charity. Let us honor all men, and not trample upon any, nor set those *among the dogs of our flock,* whom, for ought we know, Christ has set with the

1 Ecclesiastes 9:17.
2 Luke 12:51.

lambs of his. Let us never bring a railing accusation against any:[1] Michael the archangel, though he was sure in the dispute he had right on his side, and the glory of God was nearly concerned, and it was with the devil that he contended, yet he would not thus attack his adversary. The scourge of the tongue has driven more out of the temple than ever it drove into it. Let us always put the best construction on men's words and actions that they will bear, not *digging up mischief*, as evil men do, nor *rejoicing in iniquity*, but *rejoicing in the truth*, hoping the best as far as we can. Let us not aggravate matters in variance, nor by strained inuendos and misrepresentations make either side worse than it is; for that is a method which may harden one side, but can never convince the other, nor can be used with any other design but to make the contending parties hate one another; and whose kingdom that serves the interests of it, it is easy to say—not Christ's, I am sure. Let us not judge of men's spiritual and eternal state, and send men to hell presently as reprobates, because they are not in every thing of our mind, or cannot fall in with our measures. They who do so usurp a divine prerogative, take the keys of hell and death out of the hands of Christ, and show themselves to be as destitute of the fear of God, as they are of love to their neighbor.

(5.) Let us often think of the account we must

1 Jude 9.

shortly give to our great Master of all our disputes with our fellow-servants by the way. Let us consider how our disputes will look in that day, and what our own reflections will be then upon them. When the apostle asks, *Where is the disputer of this world?*[1] "Perhaps (says the excellent Archbishop Tillotson) he intends to insinuate, that the wrangling work of disputation hath place only in this world, and upon this earth, where only there is a dust to be raised; but will have no place in the other, where all things will be clear, and past dispute: and a good man would be loth to be taken out of the world reeking hot from a sharp contention with a perverse adversary, and not a little out of countenance to find himself in this temper translated into the calm and peaceable regions of the blessed, where nothing but perfect charity and good-will reign for ever."

Let our *moderation* therefore *be known unto all men*,[2] moderation in all disputes, because *our Lord is at hand;* nor let us *grudge one against another, because the Judge standeth before the door:*[3] and we may tremble to think what our doom will be, if we be found *smiting our fellow-servants;*[4] and how we shall answer it, if it be proved upon us, who have had so much forgiven us by our Master, that, for a

---

1 1 Corinthians 1:20.
2 Philippians 4:5.
3 James 5:9.
4 Matthew 24:49.

small matter, we have *taken them by the throat*.[1] But seeing we look for a day of account, in which there will be a review of disputes, let us give diligence, that we may be found of Christ in peace.[2] When Job and his friends had maintained a long dispute, in which many hasty peevish words were exchanged, God at length interposed as moderator, and gave judgment upon the debate, That they were all to be blamed, and had taken a great deal of pains (as most disputants do) to make work for repentance; and, therefore, the contending parties must ask pardon of God and one another, must forgive and forget, and live in love for the future. And this is the best end of controversies; happy were it if they were all brought to this issue now: to this issue all the controversies that are among good men will be brought at last, when they shall meet in the world of everlasting light and love.

IV. Of all disputes, Christ will be sure to reckon with his disciples for their disputes about precedency and superiority. That was the dispute here, *Who should be greatest;* and Christ does not *determine* the matter, as it might justly be expected he should have done, if he had intended that Peter, or any other of them, should have a primacy and supremacy above the rest; no, he is displeased with them for starting such a question, and disputing

1 Matthew 18:28.
2 2 Peter 3:14.

about it, because it was an indication that they all aimed at being great in the world, and were ambitious of it; and whenever preferments were to be had, they would quarrel among themselves, which should get the best; notwithstanding the meanness of their first education, when they were bred fishermen, which might have done *something* to curb aspiring thoughts; and the goodness of their late education, when they were trained up to be apostles, which might have done *much more*.

Now there are five reasons why this disposition of theirs was very displeasing to our Lord Jesus,

1. Because it came from a *mistaken notion of his kingdom*, which they had learned at the feet of their scribes, and had not yet unlearned, though they had sat so long at Christ's feet, so hard is it to conquer the power of prejudice. The Jews, misunderstanding many of the prophecies of the Old Testament, which spake of the Messiah and his kingdom; expected him to appear in external pomp and splendor, and to exercise a temporal jurisdiction, to break the Roman yoke from off their necks, and give them dominion over the neighboring nations. The disciples had imbibed this notion from infancy, and imagined (as should seem by many instances) that our Lord Jesus, though he appeared meanly at first, would soon by it thus reign; and that this was the kingdom of heaven, which they were to preach as at hand: and this they had an eye to, when they

strove who should be the greatest.

Now this was a great mistake, and the constant tenor and tendency of Christ's life and doctrine might have convinced them that it was so, that Christ's kingdom was not to be of this world,[1] but was intended to be all spiritual; the laws and powers of it, the rewards and punishments of it, all spiritual; (the weapons of our warfare are not carnal) that the Messiah was to rule by his Spirit in the spirits of men. The design of it was to refine men from the dross and dregs of worldliness and sensuality; and to raise them up to a holy, heavenly, spiritual, divine life; and to teach them to look down upon all earthly things with a gracious and generous contempt. Such as this was the constitution and complexion of Christ's kingdom, and therefore, it could not but be displeasing to him, for them to dote on earthly greatness.

2. Because it was directly contrary to the two great lessons of his school, and laws of his kingdom, humility, and love. It is against the law of humility to covet to be great in this world, and against the law of love to strive who shall be greatest. Had not Christ taught them both these lessons, both by precept and by example? Had he not made it the first condition of discipleship, that whosoever would come after him must deny themselves? Does not the great law of love oblige us in honor to prefer one

1 John 18:36.

another,[1] and to give place to our brethren? What unapt scholars then were they, who had not learned such plain and needful lessons as these! How well is it for us that we have a kind Master, who does not expel out of his school dull scholars, but gives them his Spirit to open their understandings, and bring things to their remembrance.

When we are eager in our pursuits of the world, and seek and aim at great things in it; when we are quarrelsome with our brethren, and carried out into indecencies by our contests and passions; let us think how unbecoming Christians this is, how contrary we walk to the laws of that holy religion we make profession of. And can we glory in the honor of it? Can we, with any confidence, plead the promises of it, or please ourselves with the privileges of it, or feed ourselves with the hopes of it, when we have so little regard to the precepts of it? Will those be willing to lose their lives for their religion, who cannot deny themselves the gratification of a foolish lust or passion for it?

3. Because it was utterly repugnant to the example which Jesus Christ himself had set them, and the copy he had given them to write after. The word of command which he gave them when he called them to be his disciples, was, *Follow me;* do as you see me do. But when they were disputing who should be greatest, and each setting up a title to worldly pomp

1 Matthew 16:24.

and power, they were far from resembling him, who was among them as one that served,[1] and came not to be ministered unto, but to minister.[2] The same mind should have been in them, that was in him; who was so great an example of humility and love, condescension and affection; who *emptied himself*, and *made himself of no reputation;*[3] who, not only in the general scheme of his undertaking, but in the particular passages of his life, gave such instances of self-denial, as justly are the wonder of angels; who, to teach them this lesson, and oblige them to learn it with this very argument, not long after this washed their feet, and bid them do as he had done.[4] Could the followers of such a Master contend for precedency, and not blush at the reflection upon their own folly and unworthiness?

Let us shame ourselves out of our pride, and passion, and affectation of worldly honor, and inordinate pursuit of worldly wealth, with this consideration: Shall I set my heart upon that which my Master was dead to, and denied himself in, and for my sake too? Am I not a Christian, a follower of Christ? I must then either change my name, or recover a better temper. Ought I not to walk in the same spirit, in the same steps?

---

1 Luke 22:27.
2 Matthew 20:28.
3 Philippians 2:7.
4 John 13:4–15.

4. Because it would render them very unfit for the services which he had appointed them to. It was very absurd for them to strive who should be greatest, who should live most at ease, and most in state, who should have the most power and the largest command, when they were all to labor and suffer reproach,[1] to live in meanness and poverty, to be loaded with disgrace and ignominy, and *counted as the off-scouring of all things;* nay, to *be killed all the day long,* and devoted to death, *as sheep to the slaughter,* and *ruled with rigor.* Such dispositions and expectations as these would be but a bad preparative for sufferings. They who would approve themselves good soldiers of Jesus Christ must endure hardness,[2] and not affect greatness.

And, therefore, though this infirmity, and the mistake it was grounded upon, seems by many instances after this, to have continued as long as they had Christ's bodily presence with them; yet, before they *launched out into the deep* of their service, they were perfectly cured of it, by the pouring out of the Spirit upon them; after which, we have them no more dreaming of a temporal kingdom, nor striving who should be greatest; for those whom God designs to employ in any service for him, he will either find them fit or make them so: and *as the day, so shall the strength,* so shall the

---

1 1 Timothy 4:10.
2 2 Timothy 2:3.

spirit, be. And if we would be ready for all the will of God, and stand complete in it, so as not to be driven from our work by the difficulties we may meet in it, we must be dead to worldly wealth and grandeur, and live above them, at those who look beyond them.

5. Because it was a corrupt temper that would be, more than any thing, the bane of the church in after-times; would be the reproach of its ministry, an obstruction to its enlargement, the disturbance of its peace, and the original of all the breaches that would be made upon its order and unity. Our Saviour foresaw this, and, therefore, took all occasions to check and repress it in his disciples, for a warning to all others; that all who are called by his name, and profess relation to him, may be jealous over themselves with a godly jealousy, and may look diligently, lest this root of bitterness spring up and trouble both themselves and others, and thereby many be defiled[1] and disturbed.

When we see how early in the primitive times the mystery of iniquity began to work in strifes among ministers, who should be the greatest; in Diotrephes, who loved to have the preeminence;[2] and in the man of sin, who, by degrees, under the influence of this principle, came to usurp an universal authority, and to exalt himself above all

1 Hebrews 12:15.
2 3 John 9.

that is called God, or that is worshipped;[1] let us acknowledge with what good reason Christ so often cautioned his disciples against this, and lament the mischief that is done by it to the church. It must needs be that such offenses would come; and we are told of them before, that we may not be stumbled at them; but woe to those by whom they do come. The prevalency of such a temper as this, as far as it appears, is very threatening. But when the Spirit shall be poured out upon us from on high, there shall be no more such disputes as these; and then the wilderness shall become a fruitful field.[2]

Upon the whole matter, therefore, let our strife be, Who shall be best, not who shall be greatest.

1. Let us never strive who shall be greatest in this world; who shall have the best preferment; who shall be master of the best estate, or make the best figure; but acquiesce in the lot Providence carves out to us, not aiming at great things, or striving for them.

Consider what worldly greatness is:

(1.) What a *despicable* thing it is to those who *have their eye upon another world.* All who by faith have seen the glory of God in the face of Jesus Christ, who are acquainted with the grandeur of the upper and better world, and are conversant with that world, have laid up their treasure in it,

---

1 2 Thessalonians 2:4.
2 Isaiah 32:15.

and set their hearts upon it, and hope shortly to share in the enjoyments of it; what a poor thing are the pomps and pleasures of this world to them! how easily can they write *Vanity* upon them! for they know better things. What are purple, and scarlet, and fine linen, and faring sumptuously every day, to one who is clothed with the robes of righteousness and garments of salvation, and has a continual feast upon the promises of the new covenant? What are titles of honor, or splendid attendance, to one who is called a friend of God, and about whom the holy angels encamp? What are the fading, withering glories of time, in comparison with the far more exceeding and eternal weight of glory that is to be revealed? Let us be ashamed then to strive, or seem to strive, for that which, if we act as becomes our character, we cannot but look upon with a holy contempt and indifference.

(2.) What a *dangerous* thing this worldly greatness is to those who have *not their eyes upon another world;* how apt it is to keep their hearts at a distance from God, and from the consideration and pursuit of a future blessedness; and to fix them to this world, and make them willing to take up with a portion in it: and, especially, what a strong temptation it is to break through all the sacred fences of the divine law to compass it. The devil would not have tempted Christ to worship him, with a promise of all the kingdoms of the world, and the glory of them, but that he had caught many a one with that bait. As they who will be rich, so they who will be great, and cannot think themselves happy unless they be, fall into temptation, and a snare, and into many foolish and hurtful lusts:[1] let us, therefore, never court our own trouble; nor covet to enter into temptation, as they do, who, when they are as great as God saw fit to make them, are still aiming to be greater, and striving to be greatest.

2. Let all our strife be *who shall be best*, not disputing who *has been best*, that is a vain-glorious strife, but humbly contending *who shall be so;* who shall be most humble, and stoop lowest, for the good of others; and who shall labor most for the common welfare. This is a gracious strife; a strife that will pass well in our account, when all our disputes will be reviewed. If we will covet, let us covet earnestly the best gifts,[2] covet to be rich in faith, and rich in good works. If we will be ambitious, let it be the top of our ambition to do good, and therein to be accepted of the Lord.[3] If we will aim to excel, let it be in that which is virtuous and praise-worthy, and in a holy seal for the honor of God, and the advancement of the true interests of Christ's kingdom. Herein let us strive to excel others, and to do more good than they do; not that we

---

1 1 Timothy 6:9.
2 1 Corinthians 12:31.
3 2 Corinthians 5:9.

may have the praise of it, but that God may have the glory of it, and that we may provoke others to love and to good works;[1] not that we may be many masters, but that we may make ourselves *servants of all*. Let us go before—in zeal, and yet be willing to come behind—in humility and self-denial; do better than others, and yet, in love and lowliness of mind, esteem others better than ourselves.[2]

But especially let us strive to *excel ourselves*, and to do more good than we have done. Let it be a constant dispute with our own souls, Why we do not lay out ourselves more for God. And when we remember the kindness of our youth, and the love of our espousals, instead of leaving that first love, and cooling in it, let our advanced years contend earnestly to excel our early ones, that our last days may be our best days, and our last works our best works. *Forgetting the things that are behind*, let us still *press forward* toward perfection; press forward *toward the mark, for the prize of the high calling*,[3] that at length we may have not only an entrance, but *an abundant entrance, ministered to us into the everlasting kingdom of our Lord and Saviour Jesus Christ*.[4]

---

1 Hebrews 10:24.
2 Philippians 2:3.
3 Philippians 3:13, 14.
4 2 Peter 1:11.

NOTES

NOTES

MAN'S QUESTIONS & GOD'S ANSWERS

Am I accountable to God?
Each of us will give an account of himself to God. ROMANS 14:12 (NIV).

Has God seen all my ways?
Everything is uncovered and laid bare before the eyes of him to whom we must give account. HEBREWS 4:13 (NIV).

Does he charge me with sin?
But the Scripture declares that the whole world is a prisoner of sin. GALATIANS 3:22 (NIV).
All have sinned and fall short of the glory of God. ROMANS 3:23 (NIV).

Will he punish sin?
The soul who sins is the one who will die. EZEKIEL 18:4 (NIV).
For the wages of sin is death, but the gift of God is eternal life in Christ Jesus our Lord. ROMANS 6:23 (NIV).

Must I perish?
He is patient with you, not wanting anyone to perish, but everyone to come to repentance. 2 PETER 3:9 (NIV).

How can I escape?
Believe in the Lord Jesus, and you will be saved. ACTS 16:31 (NIV).

Is he able to save me?
Therefore he is able to save completely those who come to God through him. HEBREWS 7:25 (NIV).

Is he willing?
Christ Jesus came into the world to save sinners. 1 TIMOTHY 1:15 (NIV).

Am I saved on believing?
Whoever believes in the Son has eternal life, but whoever rejects the Son will not see life, for God's wrath remains on him. JOHN 3:36 (NIV).

Can I be saved now?
Now is the time of God's favor, now is the day of salvation. 2 CORINTHIANS 6:2 (NIV).

As I am?
Whoever comes to me I will never drive away. JOHN 6:37 (NIV).

Shall I not fall away?
Him who is able to keep you from falling. JUDE 1:24 (NIV).

If saved, how should I live?
Those who live should no longer live for themselves but for him who died for them and was raised again. 2 CORINTHIANS 5:15 (NIV).

What about death and eternity?
I am going there to prepare a place for you. I will come back and take you to be with me that you also may be where I am. JOHN 14:2-3 (NIV).

www.ingramcontent.com/pod-product-compliance
Lightning Source LLC
Chambersburg PA
CBHW020439030426
42337CB00014B/1324